What *Dreams* are you *Sitting* ON

Joann Tolbert-Yancy

author of: **Romantic Secrets Men Should Know**

Editor: Daphne Hood
Cover design: Stacy Luecker
Book design: Essex Graphix
www.essexgraphix.com

Copyright © 1999, 2004 by Joann Tolbert-Yancy
All rights reserved
ISBN 0-9662501-1-7
Library of Congress Catalog Card Number: 99-095225

Second Printing

Published by JOTOSKI Publishing
P.O. Box 110691
Carrollton, Texas 75011

Printed in the United States of America

All rights reserved. No part of this book may be reproduced in any form,
in whole or in part, without written permission from the author.

For My Mentors,

Olice Richardson

John Lofton

Robert (Bob) Lewis

John Alston

Mark Clup

Ralph Hargrow

Aaron Dudley

Steve Karp

Emma Rogers

And in loving memory of my Father, Hubert Willis Lewis, and a special mentor, Terron Jackson

Table of Contents

Introduction ix

Acknowledgments xi

Finding Your "Niche" 1

Setting Your Sight 9

Self-evaluation 13

Your Plan of Action 15

It's Just Your Imagination 19

Using the Power Within 23

Mentors 27

Avoiding the "NaySayers" 31

Building Your Self-esteem 35

The Choice is Yours 39

Appendix (Self-evaluation Questionnaire) 43

Introduction

Initially when I started writing this book, I had entitled it "Leveraging Your Talent," but this title truly didn't reflect the content and message I wanted to give. So I thought maybe I should name it "Now That You Are Grown Up, Are You What You Said You Would Be." Although the second title captured the content of the book, it was a bit long. Finally, I was sitting in church and the sermon that day was "What To Do When Your Dreams Turn Into a Nightmare?" That sermon really stuck in my mind. The pastor talked about how we have dreams and we allow them to vanish because we decided to take up permanent residence in failure, heartbreak, despair and disappointment, not realizing that these things are only temporary situations. From that message I entitled this book "What Dreams Are You Sitting On." This is a perfect fit because this book is designed to help you discover your true purpose in life. My hope is that you will use the principles mentioned in this book to enhance your personal and/or professional endeavors. I truly believe that each of us has at least one God-given talent, and we should discover and use it. We came here fully equipped with everything we need to be supremely happy, successful and prosperous; and as soon as we stop looking externally for these things, the better our lives will be. Living your dream really means finding out who you are, trusting your intuition, and discovering the power within. The power within is just lying there waiting to be stirred. Once you stir your inner power, nothing can stand in your way of success. Find the courage to live your dreams. You cannot be afraid. No one will do it for you. So go ahead and give yourself permission to go after your dreams.

Acknowledgments

I am grateful, and I give thanks

To my mother, sister, brothers and family members
for affirming and supporting me.

To my sons.

To my brother Andrew for his advice and input.

To Henry Howard for his friendship
and willingness to listen.

To my friends for encouraging me to live my dreams.

What
Dreams
are you
Sitting
ON

Finding Your Niche

Every one of us is born with a talent, but most of us go through life wondering "what is my talent?" or "what is my gift?" or "what is my niche?" I have heard several answers to these questions, and they all make sense, but the answer that sticks with me the most is as simple as understanding that your talent and/or gift is something you enjoy doing. You enjoy it so much you would do it for free. It comes easy for you and difficult for others. Each time you display this talent, people always compliment you. It's a burning desire and passion that you often find yourself daydreaming about. It sets your heart on fire. This could be a combination of things, so take a moment to think about what it is that you do that brings you joy.

I remember when I first discovered my true gift. I was living in Miami, Florida. Soon after my move to the Sunshine State, I realized that the job I had was ideal; however, my working environment was terrible. It was filled with despair, insecurities and envy. Before long I became very uncertain about myself and wondered if I made the right decision by moving to Miami. This situation forced me to question my existence. Quietly I wondered about my true purpose in life. I prayed over and over for God to reveal my gift and purpose. In the back of my mind, I knew the answer; but I continued to pray for a sign or something. Then there it was staring me in my face. The year was 1995, and I was in Los Angeles with my boss and the rest of the staff implementing a company-wide training program. Our travel schedule was very aggressive. It was a one-day training with at least 85 participants. My boss would conduct the morning session and I would conduct the afternoon session. Everything was fine until it was my turn. My boss sat in the back of the room. If I uttered one sentence, my boss would say a whole paragraph from the back of the room. This went on for the entire afternoon. I was furious. The next week we were in Detroit. The training session continued as they did in Los Angeles with my boss interrupting

Finding Your Niche

every five or ten minutes. The flow of the training material was way off key, which raised my stress level to an all-time high. On our way back to the hotel, he noticed that I was very quiet and asked if I were upset. Near explosion, I blurted out, "YESSS!" By the time we arrived at the hotel, we were screaming at each other. I unloaded on that young man, and he unloaded on me. In that very instant I felt as if a great weight was lifted from my shoulder, and the knot in my stomach just disappeared.

The next morning, as we traveled back to the training site, my boss told me he wanted me to conduct the first half of the training. In my mind I felt he was trying to set me up. I knew the first half of the training, but I just hadn't done it before. I like to practice and go over the material before I present it to the class. There were ninety-two (92) participants that day. Fear gripped me, and the butterflies in my stomach were having a hoedown, foot stomping good time. I left and went to the bathroom and stood in the stall, closed my eyes and said, "Lord, Lord, Lord, I need you to guide my tongue, thoughts, and responses. Please, Father, touch the hearts, minds and souls of the people in that room so that they are open to what I have to say. Let them see you, Lord, not me. Use me as a vessel today."

I went back into that room, stood before that crowd and opened my mouth. My words flowed like a river. The participants responded, and the room was filled with a positive spirit. I was so engaged that I didn't notice that my boss never interrupted me during the session. During the first break, my boss told me he needed to get back to Miami. When I asked about the remaining training sessions, he simply said, "I am not needed here, you know what you are doing. Handle your business, young lady." And handle my business I did. I was walking and talking. People were responding and participating. It was a feeling I had never felt before. My heart was on fire. It was like a drug. After the class was over, the class stood in line to shake my hand. That night I couldn't sleep because my heart was still on fire. I couldn't wait to do the next class.

It was during my flight back to Miami when I realized my gift from God was the gift to speak. Now everything started to make sense. Some of the experiences I had in my life were things that prepared me for this wonderful gift. I remember as a little girl I was always told that I had great lungs and to turn my volume down. Today, I can speak to a room of a hundred plus people and not need a microphone because my projection is very clear and strong. I was also told early in my career that my diction was poor. Initially, I was hurt and angry, but I soon realized that maybe I should develop better diction. So I enrolled at Southern Methodist University in Dallas, Texas, for an eight-week speech and diction class. Now that I have discovered my gift and passion in life, I have a better understanding of the preparation that took place.

Finding Your Niche

Four years after my experience in Detroit, I was in Atlanta, Georgia, at the African American Women on Tour (AAWOT) Conference giving my first professional workshop presentation. I was so nervous, and the butterflies came back to visit once again. I checked in with the registration people to see how many people had signed up for my workshop. They told me that it was only 76 participants give or take two. In my mind I knew that was not enough. I wanted at least 100 people in that room because I liked speaking to large groups of people. I went downstairs and stood in the registration line and asked some of the people what workshop they were signing up for, and then I would point to my workshop and say, "I hear this one is really good and the speaker is fantastic." I stood in line and told as many people as I could. Then I went in the restaurant to encourage people to attend my workshop. When I stepped in that room the next day, 120 people were there. The people in the registration line were shocked to see that I was the speaker. I burst into laughter and promised them that they were in for a great time and experience. After the workshop, many told me I delivered on that promise.

The greatest thing you can do for yourself is to find your true purpose in life. You will never have peace of mind or ever be satisfied until you do. It doesn't matter how much money you make, how many houses or cars you own or how much you are loved. If you are not living your life's purpose, there will come a time in your life when you will ask yourself, "is this it?" or "there has to be more to life than this," or "there has to be a better way to make a living." When you get to this point in your life, you will know that you are not living your divine purpose in life. Find your divine purpose in life and do whatever it takes to live it. Your life will be fulfilled and much more productive.

You must be fully engaged, focused, exact, deliberate, relentless and steadfast; and you can only behave in this manner if you talk to your **Creator** first. Don't give up your talent and dreams to negative thinking and toxic people. They are everywhere. It could be a relative, a friend, a teacher, a preacher, a boss or a coworker— and the list goes on. But the amazing thing about living your life's purpose is that roadblocks somehow become stair steps that lead to your goal. My oldest son told me one day, "Mom, 90 percent of the people who are willing to help you, don't even know you." This is so true. Once I decided to cross that bridge of faith, every step I have made has been on solid ground, and people I never met before have been so willing to help with free information and their time.

Start seeing challenges as motivators. The minute someone tells me I can't do something, I become a full-fledged bulldog. I forget about obstacles and roadblocks. I dig my feet in and succeed. And I learn through the process and become a better person.

What I have found is that my greatest fear was not that I was

Finding Your Niche

inadequate, uninformed or not smart as others. No, my greatest fear was the power I have within me. Fear is the obstacle to our success and peace of mind. What are you afraid of? Are you afraid to live your dreams? Afraid of what people might say? Afraid to believe that you deserve to be successful, happy and prosperous? Afraid to grow? Afraid to leave your familiar surroundings? Afraid of rejection? Or are you afraid of failure? Maybe you are waiting on something. What are you waiting on? Waiting to retire? Waiting for your children to finish school? Waiting for your spouse to get a better job? Waiting until the time is right? Waiting until you have more time? Waiting until you get a promotion? Waiting to settle down? Waiting, waiting, waiting. Don't wait for some life-changing event to occur before you begin living your dreams and divine purpose in life. You will get nowhere by waiting. Take the first step and see how all that is within you will come to your assistance. Begin where you are, work where you are. Everyone who got where they are had to begin where they were. Your opportunity for success is where you are right now. Stop sitting on the side of the pool asking if the water is deep or cold. Jump in and find out for yourself. Stop wasting time.

Everything that's materialistic in this world was someone's dream or idea. So when you get up every day and go to a job that you absolutely hate, know that you are fulfilling someone else's dream.

It's very important to do something that you have a passion for, because your success is directly equivalent to the degree of happiness you get from what you do.

If you watch some of the television shows that feature the lives and lifestyles of successful people, you will find one common thread that links them all together: the love and passion for what they do.

Speaking engerizes me and sets my heart on fire. What is it that sets your heart on fire? What would you do if there were no way you could fail? What is your passion in life? What's standing in your way? What dreams are you sitting on? What's keeping you sitting on your dreams?

Stop running from your ***God-given Talent***.

Setting Your Sights

Once you have discovered your gift/talent, you must set goals to realize your dream. Yes I know, most of us hate the goal-setting process, and you can count me in that group. But when I took a closer look at the definition of a goal, my attitude changed. So what is a goal? A goal is simply a statement of intent, a target point, something to strive for or something to aim at. Goals give you a starting point and a destination. When you don't set goals, you put others in control of your career and personal life. The true purpose of a goal is to focus your attention. Once you become focused, it's hard to become distracted with things, people and situations that don't move you toward your goals. I never really appreciated goal-setting until I started to view goals as targets. You aim at targets; sometimes you hit them and sometimes you miss. When you miss, re-evaluate each goal and aim again.

In setting your goal, be clear and concise about how you want things to turn out. ("I want to complete a master's degree in computer graphics at my state university by December, 2000.") Be honest about your ability to meet your goals and make sure you have established a reasonable time frame. (If you want to be a doctor in two years, but you haven't finished high school, it is unlikely that you will achieve this goal in the time frame you have established.) As with most things, there will be challenges and obstacles along the way that can be discouraging. So it is very important that you understand what they are. The easiest way to do that is to really think about why these goals are important to you, and will they move you farther to realizing your dream. Once you have put your goals in place, analyze each one to make sure you have the skills and resources to accomplish them.

EXAMPLE

GOAL: Become a highly paid motivational speaker
STRATEGY: Generate 12 speaking engagements in 2000

Setting Your Sights

OBJECTIVES:
- Sell 5,000 copies of first book
- Gain more knowledge about public speaking
- Get a literary agent
- Send brochures to companies, local community and national organizations

SKILLS AND RESOURCES NEEDED:
- Get a literary agent
- Attend at least one seminar on public speaking
- Send brochures to the various organization
- Join a speaker's bureau

Deciding what you want is the prerequisite to getting the things that you want out of life. If you don't know where you're are going, how can you expect to get there? Wanting success isn't enough to get it. Ask yourself what you are going to do to get the things you want. Your task is to bridge the gap that exits between where you are now and the goal you intend to reach. All you need is a plan, a road map and the audacity to move on to your destination.

Self-evaluation

Self-evaluation can be a very difficult task to perform. It calls for us to lay our cards on the table and be truly honest about our weaknesses and strengths. Yet self-evaluation is a very necessary step in our self-development. One of the best tools I have found in self-evaluation is a personal questionnaire *(see Appendix)*. Customize one and give it to trusted, professional colleagues and personal friends. The main purpose of the questionnaire is to compare what you think your strengths and weaknesses are to what your colleagues and friend think. You must keep an open mind and not get upset if you hear something you don't like. That's why it is very important that you give this questionnaire to people you respect, trust and those who have your best interest at heart. In designing your questionnaire, develop questions that will give you answers that clearly show your areas of development and the areas that are strong. Please don't make this a complicated process because it really isn't. This is simply a tool. If used correctly, it will tell you what you do well and what you might want to focus more attention to developing. Also, the questionnaire might reveal talents and skills you never considered being valuable. I remember when I developed my first questionnaire and gave it to a few friends and colleagues. My first reaction was to dismiss anything that I felt was negative and not a true reflection of me. But once I got pass that initial reaction, I reminded myself to keep an open mind and view the responses as information that would help me grow. Because after all, these were people who knew a little bit about me, and I respected and trusted their opinion. It helped me form a plan of action to improve my areas of development. The reason I recommend that you solicit input from colleagues and friends is because we tend to be too judgmental and filled with criticism about ourselves. Remember your sense of humor, respect the honesty that is shared from your colleagues and friends and express your appreciation.

Plan of Action

Now that you have discovered your gift/talent and established your goals, it is time to set a plan in action. Make sure to state your objectives very clearly, limit the focus and include no more than three or four major areas in your plan. It's good to have reasonable steps so that you don't expect too much too soon and become discouraged.

In developing an action plan, there are a few things you need to include.

- **Objective:** (your objective must support your goal)

- **Action you plan to take** (these are steps that leads to your goal)
- **Who's involved** (individuals who can assist you in your efforts)
- **Target dates** (make sure they are solid but also flexible)

I have used my goal of becoming a highly paid motivational speaker in the example on the following page.

Plan of Action

Step 1

Strategy

Speaking engagements
- Sell 5000 copies of 1 book
- Gain more knowledge about public speaking
- Get a literary agent
- Mail brochures

Step 2

Action Plan

- Contact Barnes & Noble and Borders' corporate offices.
- Attend at least two seminars on public speaking and read one book on the subject
- Contact at least five agents for representation
- Send brochures and cassette tapes to women organizations, small business, friends and business associates

Step 3

Help From Others

- Author friends
- Associates who have attended speaking seminars
- Referrals from author friends
- Sons, Sister and Sisters-in-law

Step 4

Completion Date

- 12/99
- 7/99
- 9/99
- ongoing

It's Just Your Imagination

Any and everything we do starts with our imagination. Your mind is a powerful tool, so use it as your mental workshop and build anything in it that you want. Your mind is like a blueprint that guides you through this mental process that allows you to begin building your dreams. Some people call it daydreaming. When you use your imagination you are visualizing in your mind the results you want. I use visualization in every major event in my life, especially during my goal-setting process. And since I'm such a visualizer, I take scrapbooks and cut pictures out of magazines of what I'm trying to achieve.

My goal is to become a highly paid motivational speaker, so I found pictures of people sitting down facing a stage, and I took a photo of myself and placed it on that stage. This picture made everything very clear as to what I would look like and the things I would need. This was a powerful process for me because it was if I had already achieved the goal, and all I needed was the opportunity. I visualized first in my mind, every speech, presentation or workshop I have conducted. I knew exactly how I would stand, how the room would be set up and how much space I would need between me and the audience. Every detail of each event was played out first in my mind, so I increased my chances for success.

Your imagination can deliver you to success. All of us are where we are today because we first imagined it. When you stop using your imagination and dreaming, you stop living. Many people die in their minds (around 20's) and are not dead until their latter years. They just stopped dreaming. They stopped imagining that they could actually be successful or live their dreams. If you think small, you live small, and you get small results in life. The power and the opportunity to change your life is within your reach. It's not hard, it just takes effort. Start seeing things as you want them, not as they are. Your imagination will show you how to turn your dreams into reality.

Your assignment is to pick one goal that you want to

It's Just Your Imagination

visualize and twice a day spend at least 10 minutes focusing your complete attention on this goal and its outcome. Make sure you find a quiet place for focusing so you can easily concentrate. Remember this is your imagination workshop, and you are in control of everything in it. If you want to remove something, remove it. If you don't like the way things look, change them. If you need to slant an idea a certain way, do it. You are the ***BOSS***. Nothing moves until you say so. That's how powerful you are, and it is in your imagination that you create the success you want in life. Any and everything in there is there because you deem it to be. No one can remove it or take it away unless you give them permission.

Using the Power Within

I have attended many retreats, seminars and conferences that focused on empowerment. The common thread was using the power within. At first I really didn't understand this concept. What power were they speaking about? I always associated power with money, big positions in Corporate America, big homes, expensive cars or a large staff of people working for you. I soon learned that each of us has this power and inner strength just sitting there waiting to be used, and one of the ways in which we can tap into that power is by spending time with ourselves through "**Quiet Time**." The definition of quiet time means no TV, no phone, no spouse, no children, no friends, no radio—just you in a quiet place to meditate. This concept was not easy for me to get. Sitting still for five minutes or more nearly drove me crazy. But I had to tap into that inner strength, and quiet time was the only way to get there. So I tried five minutes. I started doing it during my candlelight baths. At first my mind was filled with mind chatter, and I tried to control it by focusing on the ocean or the mountains. That didn't work. A friend who had been doing quiet time for awhile, advised that I not try and get rid of the mind chatter, just let each thought flow through my mind and take deep breaths. Before long, I would be really enjoying the true meaning of quiet time. I tried this technique and now I am up to thirty- (30) minutes.

Quiet time is when I push the world out and bring *me* in, and when I bring myself in, I start by repeating my personal affirmation, "I know what I want in life and I have the courage, strength and the love for myself to do whatever it takes to get it." Then I pray. After prayer, I do what I call, "Self-talk." These talks consist of stating my best qualities and making commitments to improve myself. After the Self-talk, I lie back and enjoy the quiet.

The Quiet time process helps me to become more centered and experience inner peace. It has changed my frame of reference. I know some of you are probably saying you just

Using the Power Within

don't have the time, and your schedules are full with spouses, kids, jobs, meetings, etc., etc., etc. Please remember this: since we don't know how generous the Timegiver is going to be to us, we should be careful how we use it or allow others to use it.

Quiet time is truly a gift you give yourself, and once you treat yourself to this gift, you will gain inner strength, you will begin to trust yourself and rely more on God and your intuition. Your self-confidence will become stronger than ever before, because you have finally tapped into "THE POWER WITHIN."

Mentors

Mentors play a very important part in our personal and professional lives. But usually we don't recognize them as such. If there's a special person with whom you feel comfortable in sharing your concerns and you value their input and advice, that person is a "mentor" to you. It is essential to your success that you find and keep an ongoing mentoring relationship. So I encourage you to find a mentor. But before you start your search, here are a few concepts to consider. A true mentor encourages you to discover your purpose in life and to live it. They guide, counsel, nurture and support your efforts. They serve as a sounding board and provide the feedback you will need in your learning process. In choosing a mentor make sure there's a sense of honest communication. You need someone you can trust, someone who has the time to allow the relationship to grow and someone who will speak on your behalf in your absence. Try to have at least two mentors in order to gain different perspectives and approaches.

Remember confidentiality is the utmost of importance in a mentoring relationship.

I've had great success with my mentoring relationships. While in Miami I came to realize that I needed a mentor to help me overcome some of my career challenges. I had the technical knowledge to do my job, but I needed to develop my interpersonal skills. The person I chose was one of my boss' peers. On the surface the mentoring relationship seemed a mismatch to some because my mentor was a white male, Jewish and younger. But he proved to be the best thing that could have happened for me. My mentor was very knowledgeable of the organization, highly respected, adept in the art of organizational politics, and he had the ear of the CEO.

Although my company has a formal mentoring program in place, I chose the informal route. It allowed me to pick someone that I was comfortable with. He had the time to allow the relationship to grow, and he would be in meetings where my name would come up. If anything negative was said, he would counteract. He would present the positives about me.

He was very objective, and he didn't always agree with my approach. He challenged me. He shared the unwritten rules and gave me pointers. "Joann, you are taller than your boss. Make sure if you are standing, that you step back to eye level so he doesn't feel intimidated." He also told me that, "Whenever your boss says things that make you angry enough to want to hit him, come to my office and cuss me out instead." My mentor had my best interest at heart, and what I said never left the room. Through it all he never said a negative word about my boss. His focus was on making me better, showing me ways to handle difficult situations, forcing me to see the "big picture" and making me dig deep inside my soul to bring forth the best of me. One of the greatest pieces of advice he gave me about how best to achieve professional success was to continue believing in myself when no one else would and learn how to be okay with myself. I am eternally grateful to that young man. I still call on him for advice. I believe he learned from me, too.

I have experienced many wonderful mentoring relationships throughout my career and personal life. Each one of them has been a cornerstone in my life for guidance, support and encouragement. I've learned how to be a mentor and currently mentor three people. Take this part of your development very seriously and choose wisely.

Avoiding the "Naysayers"

Naysayers are people we know, love and are near and dear to our hearts. They are easily recognized by the words they say and the things they do.

Once you make it known that you have a dream and intend on pursuing it, the naysayers will be standing along the side of the road as you journey toward your dream shouting out how stupid your ideas sound. They will be filled with advice about what you should do and what you can't do. Don't fool yourself into thinking that naysayers are strangers. Most of time they are relatives or friends. Some of them really don't mean any harm; it's just that they can't see past their own limitations, so they place them on you. But there are those who do mean harm. They are discouraging, and negative thinking people, and all they want to do is to control you. But once you set your goals and become focused, the things they say will slide right off because you have developed a "TEFLON MENTALITY" (nothing negative will stick)

The best way to avoid the naysayers is by surrounding yourself with people who are doing what you want to do. When I decided to write my first book, I heard all kinds of negative things from people who had no idea what it took to write or publish a book. So I starting associating with published authors and visiting bookstores to get referrals. They made it easy for me and gave valuable information freely.

So, if you want to soar like an eagle you can't hang around with chickens, pigeons and buzzards. Which reminds me of that old story I heard that really brings this thought home. It's about the eagle that lost one of her eggs. A hen found it in the barnyard and took it to the chicken coop and sat on it with all the love and care she could find. A few weeks later the egg hatched and out stepped a tiny eagle in the barnyard. This tiny bird had an eagle history, eagle genes, eagle power and eagle potential. But because he was living in a chicken environment, he lost his identity. He did not know who he was, so he grew up thinking he was a chicken, dreaming chicken dream, having

Avoiding the "Naysayers" 33

little chicken thoughts, playing chicken games, and entertaining chicken ambitions. In fact, he was made to feel ashamed of his eagle beak. Even though he did not know who he was, the other chickens in the barnyard knew, and they knew he was different. They didn't want him to know. They were afraid he would eventually rise above them and rule over them. So they tried to keep him in the dark.

Some people don't want you to know who you are; and they don't want you to realize your true gifts and talents. So this little eagle became ashamed of his eagle heritage and eagle features. The chickens would make fun of his mighty beak because they had little thin narrow beaks. They made fun of his eagle talents and his claws. He became ashamed of the richness of his dark eagle feathers. In fact, at one point he even considered having cosmetic surgery. He thought about cutting off half his eagle beak and dyeing his dark eagle feathers so he could look more like a chicken. His greatest ambitions were to hop and skip around like a rooster and climb up on a fence and cock-a-doodle-do.

But one day while this little confused bird was playing in the barnyard, he saw the dark contours of a mighty adult eagle flying above him. For the first time in his life this eagle looked higher than the fence and beyond the chicken environment. For the first time in his life he saw an adult eagle with all of his majesty, grace and power. In other words, he saw the potential that was in him; he saw what he was able to become. He became transfixed on this beautiful creature and he said, "I want to be like that." He started feeling this rush in his soul calling him beyond who he was, calling all that chicken stuff out of him. And as he was feeling this rush, the adult eagle swooped down to him and said, "Hey boy, you are not a chicken. You are an eagle. Come on and spread those beautiful dark wings and fly with me so we can get out of this barnyard environment.

Take an inventory of your environment. What kind of birds are you hanging out with?

Building Your Self-Esteem

What is self-esteem anyway? Self-esteem is simply the value we place on ourselves.

Have you ever seen someone who has high self-esteem? They stand out in crowd with their heads and shoulders up and look you straight in the eye when talking to you. You know just by watching them that they feel good about themselves; they are focused and know what they want out of life. It feels good being around them because they always have encouraging words to say and in the back of your mind you are hoping that their spirit will somehow rub off on you. Do you wonder how they got that way? Well there are no magic wands that grant high self-esteem, you have to build it. The first step in building high self-esteem is to understand how it works. Self-esteem centers on your thoughts. If you think you are stupid and ugly it will be reflected in your behavior. You will lack self-confidence, have an unhappy personal life, make everyone around you miserable, blame everyone for your mistakes and your body, mind and spirit will suffer. However, if your thoughts are positive, that, too, will be displayed. With high self-esteem and good feelings about yourself, you welcome challenges, learn from your mistakes, become more flexible. Your self-confidence is stronger and stays intact. If you start right at this very moment to trust your intuition, nurture yourself, become interdependent and allow your identity to grow, you will be on the right road to building a healthy self-esteem.

Not too long ago I was sharing with a friend that my spirits were low, and I just couldn't seem to focus on anything. He told me that he used to feel like that until he realized that he was the greatest person he knew. Initially I thought he sounded a little egotistical, but he explained that God had blessed him with so much (intelligence, good looks, good heart and a caring spirit) that it would be crazy to think anything different. Then he asked me a very simple question, "If you saw yourself walking down the street, what impression would you get just by watching yourself?" I thought for a second and said, "Well,

Building Your Self-esteem

friendly, smartly dressed, handsome woman, self-assured, a lot of presence, focused, kind facial expressions," and my list went on. I thought about the adjectives that I used to describe myself and quickly realized that I had nothing to be depressed about because I had been wonderfully blessed. Needless to say, my spirits were lifted as I continued to focus on what was good about me and not what I thought was wrong or negative.

Because self-esteem is crucial to your success, here are a few ways in which you can increase your self-esteem.:
- Determine your positive characteristics (*i.e. your smile, your hair, intelligence, skills, etc.*)
- Don't compare yourself with others
- Appreciate your achievements and credentials
- Go ahead, feel proud of yourself (*not in an egotistical way*)
- Start a "Gratitude Journal" and each day write down at least five (5) things for which you are grateful
- Become a mentor (*Big Brother & Big Sister organization*)
- Consider volunteering at least once a week (*nursing homes or children's ward at your local hospitals*)
- Incorporate at least ten minutes of "Quiet Time" in your schedule to meditate
- Review your personal and professional goals daily in

order to stay focused
- Learn to trust yourself
- Learn something new
- Treat yourself to something special (*i.e. dinner, movies, massages, or a weekend getaway*)
- Set aside one night a week *(30 minutes to an hour) for* "pampering" *(long candlelight bath while listening to your favorite songs and sipping your favorite beverage)*
- Listen to motivational tapes and up beat music
- Learn to laugh and laugh a lot

Building your self-esteem will not be an easy task, and there are no shortcuts. You have the power and ability to raise your own self-esteem by beginning to value yourself. Become aware of what your inner voices tell you in good and distressed situations. Become open and willing to grow and imagine yourself being successful. Remember you can lift or lower your self-esteem by your thoughts.

The Choice Is Yours

The choice really is yours. There is one gift God gave all of us and that is the gift of choice. Even if you decide to do nothing with your gift, talents or dreams it's clear that it's your choice to do nothing. Think about this for a moment, we are our choices and we live our choices. We are where we are today because we chose to be, and whenever we decide we want change in our lives at any given point or time, change will happen. It's that simple. If it's success you want, choose it. It will always be your decision. Don't allow others to make your choices in life because you will have to live with these decisions. Since choice is directly connected to "making a decision," a lot of us get cold feet and talk ourselves out of truly making an effort to live our dreams.

Before I really understood the power of choice, I was miserable. I tried to be everything people thought I should be. My mind was cloudy, and it was hard for me focus. I learned the power of choice very early. It started when I became a mother at age sixteen. I was able to conceal my pregnancy in order to complete my junior year. After my son was born, I tried to enroll in school, but was told that I would have to wait until my son was at least a year old before the school board would consider allowing me to finish my senior year. This was a very painful thing for me to hear because I truly enjoyed school, and it meant that I would not graduate with my class. I was blessed with wonderful, loving parents who saw my determination and allowed me to attend school in another town while they kept my son. It was at that moment I decided that I was worth the effort and that my son deserved everything I had to give. I did finish school the same time as my class in a different town. It would have been easy to wait for the school board to allow me back in school, but I chose another route and accomplished the same results. Since then I have made many choices in my life, some good, some not so good, but they were my choices to make.

Two years ago I made the choice to live my dream. I set

The Choice Is Yours

my goals and put my action plan in place. It has been the most rewarding thing I have ever experienced. The more choices I make that pushes me closer to my goals and dreams the more I understand the dynamics behind the power of choice.

So when you find yourself at work upset about things you cannot change, you choose to be upset. When you put your dreams on hold, you choose to, when you stay in abusive relationship, you choose to stay, when you didn't go back to finish school, you choose not to, when you find yourself around negative people and negative environments, you choose to be, if you are not growing and developing yourself, you choose not to, if you are in a relationship, personal or professional, that is not going anywhere, you choose to stay.

Ahhhhh! But when you choose to stop sitting on your dreams, you will; when you choose to find your true purpose in life, you will; when you choose to set your goals, you will; when you choose to use the power within, you will and when you choose to build your self-esteem, you will. Finally, when you choose to live your dream and find that your life is fulfilled, productive and prosperous, you will know that you made the right choice. I once heard a wise man say that if you choose to pray to the HIGH GOD OF POVERTY, He will lavish you, because if you want nothing, you will get plenty of it. That is why you must see the power of choice as a magnificent gift.

What choices are you making that will lead to your divine purpose in life and stop you from sitting on your dreams?

Appendix
Self-evaluation Questionnaire

1. **What is it like to work with him/her.**

2. **List their strengths.**

    1.

    2.

    3.

    4.

3. **List their weaknesses.**

   1.

   2.

   3.

   4.

4. **What do you think is his/her greatest talent?**

5. **How does he/she treat others?**

6. **How do others treat him/her?**

7. **Does he/she work well with others? Why or why not?**

8. **Is he/she good at his/her job?
   Explain:**

Appendix

9. Is he/she a team player, loner, leader, rebel?
   Explain:

10. Does he/she have a well-groomed physical appearance?

11. In your opinion, what aspects of his/her physical appearance needs work?

12. How do others see him/her?

13. If you had an opportunity, what advice would you pass on to him/her?

About the Author

Joann Tolbert-Yancy, a native of Arkansas, has spent 23 years as a Human Resources professional for various major corporations.

Joann does what few speakers/facilitators can do effectively. She manifests to an audience the depth of knowledge in the areas of employment, law and career development, all blended into a dynamically compelling presentation.

Her style of deliverance is energetic, powerful and thought provoking. She has literally had workshop participants and audience members sitting on the edge of their seats, and she creates an environment that encourages everyone to participate.

If you would like to book Ms. Tolbert-Yancy
for future engagements, please contact her at:

**JOTOSKI Publishing
P.O. Box 110691
Carrollton, Texas 75011**

Or call: **(972) 418-1491**

Also by Joann Tolbert-Yancy
Romantic Secrets Men Should Know
An intriguing collection of ideas to enhance any romantic endeavor.

Notes

Notes

JOTOSKI Publishing